The Professional Radical

Conversations with

SAUL ALINSKY

Marion K. Sanders

The Professional

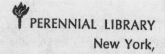

PERENNIAL LIBRARY
New York,

Radical

Conversations with

SAUL ALINSKY

Harper & Row, Publishers
Evanston and London

THE PROFESSIONAL RADICAL:
Conversations with Saul Alinsky

The essays in this book originally appeared in *Harper's Magazine* in the June 1965, July 1965, and January 1970 issues. They are here reprinted by arrangement.

First PERENNIAL LIBRARY edition published 1970 by Harper & Row, Publishers, Inc.
49 East 33rd Street, New York, N.Y. 10016.

LIBRARY OF CONGRESS CATALOG CARD NUMBER: 74–115185

Contents

Contents

Introduction to Part One

Known today as this country's foremost organizer of community action groups, Chicago-born Saul Alinsky was trained as a criminologist. Early in his career he was caught up in the radical movements of the Thirties and joined John L. Lewis in the tumultuous birth throes of the CIO. However, despite his enduring admiration for Lewis (whose biography he wrote in 1949), he was convinced that his own role was outside of the labor movement. His first proving ground was the grim slum where Chicago's stockyard workers lived in the hate-ridden squalor immortalized earlier in Upton Sinclair's *The Jungle*. In this unlikely setting, Alinsky forged a coalition of workers, small merchants, union leaders and local churches. Using sit-downs, boycotts and other militant tactics, the Back of the Yards Council won major concessions from City Hall and at the same time mounted a self-help program which transformed the area into a model working-class community.

Alinsky's unabashed aggressiveness affronted the benevolent liberals who then, as now, dominated the social-welfare and business establishments. But his effectiveness in combating both native fascist and Communist influences won him the support of Bishop Bernard J. Sheil, one of the most progressive Catholic prelates of his day. Sheil introduced Alinsky to Marshall Field III. As his biographer, Stephen Becker, has described the encounter, the Protestant millionaire was immediately drawn to this son of Jewish immigrants who had "succeeded in transforming a traditional concern for justice and learning, and a traditional capacity for endurance, into an active, even truculent, genius for social reform."

Field offered Alinsky a subsidy which would enable him to carry his ideas and methods to other areas where the Back of the Yards pattern might succeed. Persuaded after considerable debate that his freedom of action would be unhampered, Alinsky accepted and in 1940 the Industrial Areas Foundation was created with sufficient capital to pay him a modest salary and, in due course, to recruit a small staff. As a free-lance professional agitator, he went to work in cities across the country. The going proved rough. For a while he carried a business card reading, "Have trouble, will travel." During numerous stays in local jails he wrote his book *Reveille for Radicals*—a personal credo which Jacques Maritain called "epoch making." Maritain, who subsequently became a warm personal friend, introduced Alinsky to the Archbishop of Milan—now Pope Paul VI—with whom he spent a week in Italy discussing the Church's relationship to local communist unions. "It was an interesting experience," he recalls, "between Archbishop Montini and a beautiful grey-eyed, blonde Milanese Communist union official with whom I explored common interests bridging Communism and capitalism."

I first met Alinsky in 1964 when he had begun to surface as a figure of national importance after Charles E. Silberman, in his book *Crisis in Black and White*, characterized the Woodlawn Organization known as TWO, which Alinsky nurtured in a Chicago ghetto, as "the most significant social experiment going on among Negroes in America today." To see Alinsky in person is something of a shock. For this firebrand is a tall, grey-haired, squarely-built, bespectacled, and conservatively dressed man who looks less like a practising revolutionary than a bemused professor of philosophy. Blessed with a rare combination of reckless wit and cool detachment, his gestures and language are muscular, whether he is using the idiom of metaphysics or the vernacular of the streets. He is at home with both.

At that time, following a tragic race riot, churches in Rochester, New York had invited him to go to work in their black ghetto. To the considerable dismay of the local establishment, he accepted. Anticipating his arrival, the press described Rochester as "a city set on edge." Elsewhere—in the words of one journalist, his presence evoked "screams of rage, moans and groans. He provokes violent reactions—apparently it is impossible to be neutral about him."

Among his bitterest critics was Dr. Harold Fey, then editor of *Christian Century*, who accused him of fomenting "a political movement whose object is to establish control over urban society by raising up from its ruins a 'power structure' dictatorship based on slum dwellers." Another adversary, Julian Levi of the University of Chicago, charged him with emulating the techniques of "lynch mobs."

Alinsky passes off such comments with an ironic shrug. The problem, he says, is that—unlike his critics—he really believes in democracy. We discussed these and many other ideas —along with his life and times—at length in the early months of 1965. The narrative that follows was excerpted from a tape recording of those conversations.

M.K.S.

The Making of an Anti-Fascist

How did I get started? Where did I come from? Chicago. I can curse and hate the town but let anyone else do it and they're in for a battle. There I've had the happiest and the worst times of my life. It's the only place on earth where I've cried. Every street has its personal joy and pain to me. When I go to watch the Cubs or the Bears play and turn off on Addison Street, it isn't just that. On this street is the church of a Catholic bishop who was a big part of my life; farther down is another church where the pastor too has meant a lot to me; and a couple of miles away is a cemetery—well, skip it. Many Chicago streets are pieces of my life and my work. Things that happened there have rocked boats in a lot of cities. Nowadays, I fly all over the country in the course of my work. But when those flaps go down over the Chicago skyline, I know I'm home.

I was born in one of the worst slums in Chicago. It's still there but urban renewal has changed it into an orderly jungle—a public housing project. We were poor—my parents were Russian immigrants, Jewish and very orthodox. My mother still keeps a kosher house. She was only seventeen when she had me. As a kid I remember always living in back of a store. My idea of luxury was to live in an apartment where I could use the bathroom without one of my parents banging on the door for me to get out because a customer wanted to get in.

In my work it's been one "Look Homeward, Angel!" after another. I suppose it's because nearly all the places where I used to live are now slums taken over by Negroes or Mexican-Americans or Puerto Ricans. A couple of months ago I talked at a meeting on the West Side of Chicago. It was in one of my old neighborhoods which is now all Negro, and the meeting was in a Baptist church which used to be a synagogue. I was Bar Mitzvahed there. I remembered it as being the size of the Roman Colosseum but now I saw it was just a little box of a place.

My parents were divorced when I was thirteen or fourteen and my father moved out to California and did pretty well after a while. I was supposed to live with him part of the time. When I first went West to Los Angeles he was living in a Jewish neighborhood called Boyle Heights. Years later when I went back to help organize Mexican-Americans there I was right back in Boyle Heights again.

Most people spend their lives working their way up. But I seem to have been working my way down. Still, who's to say which is really up or really down?

Anyway, I didn't see much of my father except to say, "Hello," and three months later to say, "Goodbye." Out there I lived alone. It was an oddball sort of life. I was shacked up with an old bag of twenty-two. When you are sixteen or seventeen, twenty-two is really old. Between moving around with my mother in Chicago and different summer schools out West I must have gone to a dozen different high schools. When I finally graduated from Hollywood High they sent my credits back to the other schools and I wound up with three or four high-school diplomas.

As a kid I don't remember being bothered by a social conscience. Out West I was mad about tennis like the other kids but I never amounted to much in that. Back in Chicago I got obsessed with aviation. I was convinced that it was going to be big stuff and when that happened I wanted to be in the middle of it. On weekends I'd take the elevated out to Checkerboard Air Field. I'd sweep up the hangars, run errands, do anything just so they'd teach me to fly. In those days they were flying the airmail by following the Lincoln Highway. I worked for Yackey's Aircraft, which took people up—ten bucks for ten minutes. One day I saw Tony Yackey killed testing a little sport job he had put together—a T.M. with an OX5 motor—and I decided to be an aeronautical engineer instead of a pilot.

I entered the University of Chicago in 1926. More or less by accident, I majored in archaeology and I fell in love with the subject. It was all very exciting and dramatic to me. The artifacts were not just pieces of stone or clay. My imagination could carry me back to the past so that when I stood in front of an old Inca altar I could hear the cries of human sacrifices. You need a lot of imagination to be a good organizer. Today when I go into a community, I suffer and resent with the people there, and they feel this. It's a big thing in my relationships.

In college I took a lot of sociology courses too, but I can't say they made a deep impression on me. Jim Farrell once wrote—I think it was in *Fortune*—that the sociology department of the University of Chicago is an institution which spends $100,000 on research programs to find out the location of houses of prostitution which any taxi driver could tell them for nothing.

In the sociology department it was a cardinal sin to make a categorical statement. You qualified everything you said; then you qualified the qualifiers and added some footnotes so that the final conclusion had more escape hatches in it than a loan shark's mortgage contract. Today the University of Chicago sociology department is just a tribe of head counters.

Well, when I started working with people I found them asking, "Is it yes or no? Do we go this way or that?" So I had a lot of unlearning to do when I got out of college—including the fancy vocabulary I'd picked up. This is not so easy. When you get your degree you can't wear it around your neck to prove you're educated. So instead you use a lot of three- and four-syllable words. Of course, they aren't any use at all if you really want to communicate with people. You have to talk straight English, using a small word every time you can instead of a big one.

When I was in my third or fourth year of college, some of the students got interested in the coal miners in southern Illinois who were rebelling against John L. Lewis and the United Mine Workers Union. We collected some food and chartered a couple of trucks and drove down there to help the starving coal miners. I had a run-in with one of those small-town sheriffs and I got pinched—the first of a whole series of arrests, though it was a new experience for me then. It's ironic—my plunge into social action was to fight John L. Lewis. Later he took a great liking to me.

I learned a lot about organizational tactics watching him and working with him in the early days of the CIO. Many things that happen during an organizing drive are utterly unplanned and the biggest job of a leader is to develop a rationale, a moral basis for these spontaneous actions. For instance, when the first sit-down strikes took place in Flint, no one had really planned them. They were clearly a violation of the law—trespass, seizure of private property. Labor leaders ran for cover, refused to comment. But Lewis issued a pontifical statement, "A man's right to a job transcends the right of private property," which sounded plausible. It undergirded the sit-downs with a purpose, a direction. If he hadn't done this the strikes might well have collapsed and the Auto Workers' organizing drive would have failed.

This is one of many great lessons Lewis taught me. But it's not the kind of stuff you learn in college.

I graduated—*cum laude* I guess—in 1930. The Depression was on and archaeology was as dead as the subject matter. Who was going to subsidize archaeological expeditions in a time of economic depression? So I couldn't get any kind of a job except some of that make-work stuff around the

University where you slice the ragged edges off maps and get paid about ten cents an hour. I didn't need much money the way I was living. I had this Swedish landlady who would say, "Forget about it; pay me when you can." My problem was eating. I knew my mother would gladly give me her last dollar and the last crumb on her table. But she was having a hard time and my father had more or less disappeared from sight. So I'd tell her I had enough. I could have gone on a relief project. But I don't know why this is— I'll steal before I'll take charity.

For a while I solved my eating problem by going into a big deluxe food store where they gave out free samples—little pieces of Danish ham and cheese and so forth. At the dessert counter they always had junket. I guess I ate junket for a month. Then one day two guys came alongside of me and tossed me out on the street—just like one of those old movie comedies. That was the end of that.

Soon after that I was having a cup of coffee in a cheap restaurant—one of a chain. I was meditating, "Here I am such a smart son of a bitch, *cum laude* and all that—how come I can't make a living? I've given society a chance. I've tried a number of legitimate ways. Where do I go from here?"

Then I got an idea. I took my cup of coffee and sat down next to the cashier and chatted with her. Then I got up to go and said, "I'm sorry, I've lost my check." She saw I'd only had a cup of coffee; so she said, "Well that'll be a nickel," and gave me a check. I paid that one and walked four blocks to another restaurant in the same chain with the original nickel check in my pocket. I ate a meal that cost about a buck forty-five—and believe me in those days you could practically buy the fixtures in the joint for that price. I paid the five-cent check when I left.

Well, my economy was settled. I could eat for a nickel a day. But then I began to have trouble. I guess you could call it the stirrings of a social conscience. All around the university I saw kids who were in the same boat I was. They were hungry. I found I couldn't keep my big secret to myself. So I put up a sign on one of the bulletin boards inviting anyone who was hungry to a meeting. Well, some of them thought it was a gag. But they came. The place was really jumping. I explained my system, using a big map of Chicago with all the chain restaurants spotted on it—my first practical use of social ecology. I divided them in teams to work the North Side one day and the South Side the other. This went on for about six months. Then all the restaurants installed those little serial machines that stand at the door and you pull out a ticket which is only good in that one place. Automation. Well that finished us.

Then I discovered a very interesting thing. All those kids kept after me asking, "What do we do now?" When I said I didn't know they resented it. There's an old saying about favors extended becoming defined as rights. I found out it's true.

One morning I opened up my mailbox and there was an official letter from Robert Maynard Hutchins, the president of the university, informing me that I had been awarded the Social Science Graduate Fellowship in Criminology. This was a fellowship that carried your tuition and your room and board and waived you through your master's to your doctorate. Why I got it I don't know. I never took a course in criminology and I had only the most casual kind of acquaintance with Hutchins. He'd only been president a year when I graduated. We're good friends now, even though I have a lot of reservations about what goes on in lofty towers whether they're on Morningside Heights or the hills of Santa Barbara—far away from people. I suppose some good—maybe even some important things come out of this *luftmensch* stuff. But I live in a different kind of world.

My assignment as a graduate student was to get insight into crime. I figured the way to do this was to get inside. So I went over to the hotel which everybody knew was the headquarters of the Capone gang. I found one of the characters whose picture I'd seen in the papers and said to him, "I'm Saul Alinsky and I'm studying criminology at the University of Chicago. Do you mind if I hang around with you?" He looked at me and said, "Get lost, punk." The same thing happened several times.

Then one day I was sitting alone in a restaurant. At the next table was one of Capone's top gunmen—I won't mention his name because he may be a big Rotarian now. He had six or seven pals around him and he was saying, "Hey you guys, did I ever tell you about the time I picked up that redhead in . . ." A moan went up around the table. "My God, do we have to hear that one again?"

So I leaned over and plucked his sleeve and said, "Mister, I'd love to hear that story." "You would, kid?" he said. "Pull up a chair." That's the way it went. He had an audience for his stories. He introduced me to Frank Nitti and other people and from then on I was okay with the Capone gang. They knew exactly what I was doing. I was their total student body—they'd kid each other and say, "Hey, Professor, you take over the class." I think it had a certain appeal to their egos.

Anyhow they knew that if I wanted to talk, there was no one to talk to. They owned City Hall, they owned the federal agencies. Maybe I shouldn't say owned. They had their arrangements with the Democratic party and the Republican party. Why, when one of those guys got knocked off, there wasn't any court in Chicago. Most of the judges were at the funeral and some were pallbearers.

I found out that life is pretty mixed up, that you had to strain to tell who was better than whom. Because here was this criminal gang and here were all the good people who were the market for booze, for dames, for gambling. I came to see the Capone gang as a huge quasi-public utility servicing the population of Chicago. The Capone outfit had really gone public; everyone had stock in it. And the gangsters were the major contributors to charities. When Capone showed up at a Northwestern football game on Boy Scout Day, three thousand Scouts got up and yelled, "Yea Al." That's character building for you.

In the Capone gang I learned, among other things, the terrific importance of personal relationships. Nitti once explained to me why from time to time they were hiring out-of-town killers. It's one thing, he said, to go up to a guy you don't know. You've been told he'll be wearing a dark-gray hat and coat, and so forth. You walk up to him in a crowd and put the gun up against his belly and you let him have a couple and fade off. That's doing a job. But if the killer knows the other guy, when he puts it up against his belly he suddenly looks up and sees his face, he knows his wife, he's taken his kids to the ball game, he knows that if he pulls that trigger there's going to be a widow, kids without a father, there'll be tears, there'll be a funeral—then it becomes murder. It isn't a job anymore, and he's going to hesitate, and maybe not even do it. That was the reason they used out-of-town killers.

This is what sociologists call a "primary relationship." They spend lecture after lecture and all kinds of assigned reading explaining it. Professor Nitti taught me the whole thing in five minutes.

At the end of my second year in graduate school a job with the State Division of Criminology suddenly opened up. I left the University and took the position, figuring I'd come back and do my doctor's some other time. Well, that was the end of that. I never went back, or even gave it another thought. My new bosses wanted me to continue with the Capone thing. But I felt I'd had it. I'd learned about all I was going to learn out of this situation. I was more interested in the young kids, the "Forty-two" gang, which was held responsible at that time for 80 per cent of the auto thefts in Chicago. These were mostly Italian kids who were just moving into the rackets. I wanted to study them, so the State Division made this my first assignment. It was much harder than getting in with the Capone gang because these kids were very suspicious.

They did not have any fixes or deals with the authorities and they were pretty quick on the trigger. I hung around and after a while they got used to it. Sometimes I would overhear things and they knew I overheard it, and they watched and waited to see if the cops were going to hear about it and move in. I got pretty nervous too because if by some fluke the cops had moved in on something like that, then I would have gotten the rap. But I was lucky and we got to know each other as people.

I've seen this kind of thing operate over and over again. Take the well-known anti-Semitic cliché, "Some of my best friends are Jews." To the guy who says this, the Jews he knows really *are* his good friends. His prejudices are over on this stereotype that he has way out there.

But let me qualify this. I've also learned that when it comes to conflict, a personal relationship cannot substitute for a power relationship. I discussed this with George Romney when he was president of American Motors just before he went for the governorship of Michigan. I like him. He has good instincts. He'd been giving me a big deal about how he and Walter Reuther go to Great Books things together, and have Aspen-type, Santa Barbara-type discussions. Finally I said, "Look, that's all to the good, but when negotiations time comes, Reuther will walk in and you'll be on a first-name basis. He'll say, 'Look, George, I hate to do this to you, but we've got to have that raise. You're the last guy in the world I'd want to shut down but my membership insists on it and you're either gonna come across or you're gonna get shut down.'" Romney smiled reminiscently and we never talked about it again.

I learned more about human relationships on my next job, which was as a criminologist at the state prison in Joliet. I worked there for three years. When we had to electrocute an inmate everybody would be half-tanked, including the warden. It's one thing for a judge and jury to sit there for two weeks condemning a guy who doesn't even have a personality. He's just a defendant. But after he'd been in prison eight months or so—between stays and reprieves and hearings—we got to know him. We got to know his kids. By the time he went to the chair we weren't executing a convicted felon. We were murdering a human being.

A prison is a restricted society where everybody's motivations are plainly visible, even when they try to use rather subtle tactics. I remember one inmate—a lifer—saying to me that the inmates really ran the joint even though the authorities thought *they* did. That was true.

The trouble with working in an institution is that you get institutionalized—callous. You stop thinking. I saw this was happening to me after a couple of years. I would be interviewing an inmate and I no longer had any real curiosity as to why this particular guy did what he did. I knew then that it was time for me to get out.

There were other reasons too. I've never encountered such a mass of morons as in the field of criminology. Anyone who has a shadow of intelligence becomes a national authority—which I was by the time I was twenty-four or twenty-five. They never read anything outside of their own field. I remember once quoting John Strachey in a talk and afterward a couple of big officials asked me what prison Strachey was warden of.

I was doing a certain amount of lecturing at sociological conferences and at colleges as well as my prison job. I was more or less in the academic world. Though I wasn't satisfied with what I was doing, my main reason for staying was that even though my income was low I had my "integrity." You must remember that this was before the days when being on a faculty or the staff of an institution gave you a sort of license to practice as a consultant, coordinator, or government adviser. We just had our modest pay checks—no consulting fees, no fringe benefits—plus our "integrity." I figured if I went into business I'd have to be buttering up my customers, agreeing with them politically, and so forth. While in the academic field you could be honest, and the price you paid for this luxury was a low salary.

Well, I found out I was wrong. In criminology or any academic field you're dependent on foundation grants, on university trustees, on public authorities. You're not supposed to get involved in controversy or public issues or you will become known as a "troublemaker" or as someone who has "personality difficulties."

In criminology, for instance, all the experts agreed that the major causes of crime were poor housing, discrimination, economic insecurity, unemployment, and disease. So what did we do? We went in for supervised recreation, camping programs, something mysterious called "character building." We tackled everything but the actual issues. Because the issues were controversial. Sometimes I'd say, "Come on, let's stop this crap, we know what the causes of crime are." Then they'd say, "Don't be radical."

After a while I saw that the only difference between being in a professional field and in business was the difference between a ten-buck whore and a hundred-dollar call girl.

While I was going through this disillusionment, all hell was breaking loose around the world. Hitler was taking over Europe; Japan was on the march; Mussolini was moving into Ethiopia, and when Litvinov opened his mouth to protest about it at the League of Nations, Halifax would answer by politely belching in his face. Then the Spanish Civil War broke loose and the Fascists were using it to test out their newest weapons and tactics. In this country the New Deal was under way and the CIO was starting to roll.

With so much happening I found I couldn't keep my mind on a kid sitting across the desk from me who had stolen an automobile or burglarized a store.

So I started doing my job as a sort of sinecure. I quit right when quitting time came and I got involved in raising money for the International Brigade, for the sharecroppers down South, helping stop the evictions of city people who couldn't pay rent, fighting for public housing. Wherever you turned you saw injustice. The issues stuck out as clearly as they did in a prison. You knew what was good and what was evil. Life was very exciting. I remember one stunt that went very well—I organized poker parties to raise money for the Newspaper Guild and the International Brigade. I'd found out that you can only appeal directly to people on issues once or twice. But if they're gambling, it's within their experience to take a little out of the pot for a good cause. They can feel noble while they're playing poker.

I met plenty of Communists in those days. Anyone who was involved in the causes of the 'thirties and says he didn't know any Communists is either a liar or an idiot.

I was sympathetic to Russia at that time because it was the one country that seemed to be taking a strong position against Hitler. I hated the Nazis with a deep, deep passion. My one regret about the Bomb—to this day—is that it wasn't dropped on Berlin instead of Hiroshima and Nagasaki. If you were anti-fascist on the international front in those days you had to stand with the Communists. And in this country they were all over the place fighting for the New Deal, for the CIO, and so forth.

But I never joined the Party. Matter of fact I've never joined any organization—not even the ones I've organized myself. So far as the Communists went, there were several special things that kept me out. Partly it was philosophic. One of my articles of faith is what Justice Learned Hand called "that ever-gnawing inner doubt as to whether you are right." I've never been sure I'm right but I'm also sure nobody else has this thing called truth. I hate dogma. People who believed they owned the truth have been responsible for the most terrible things that have happened in our world, whether they were Communist purges or the Spanish Inquisition or the Salem witch hunts. The Communists I knew were doctrinaire and rigid. I had learned that you had to look at life in a flexible, fluid way. I also knew that in this kooked-up irrational world, you really have to have a sense of humor to survive. And doctrinaire people have no humor.

I remember one big CIO protest meeting, after the Little Steel massacre. The top officials of the CIO were there including the director of the Communist party of Illinois. He was giving a nonstop speech about bloody-handed murderers and capitalists and Little Steel and Tom Girdler. I left and went across the street to have a bite to eat. As I was going out, he was saying, "And in conclusion, Comrades, let me tell you . . ." When I came back about twenty-five minutes later, he was still talking. Saying the same stuff over again. Some guys sitting near me were well-known Communists. They had been very friendly, so I said, "You know, for the first time I understand why they shoot these sons of bitches in Russia." They looked at me as if I was a leper. There wasn't a shred of humor among them.

A lot of my liberal friends did join the Communist party. At the time it didn't seem too important. But now I see that what the Communists did to them and others like them has hurt this country much more than the things J. Edgar Hoover talks about. Every generation in America has had its radicals who were willing to stand up and fight. Then, in the 1950s, McCarthy made this country a graveyard of fear. And men who had joined the Communist party when they were youngsters were terrified, and tried to bury themselves in respectable middle-class suburban life.

So the Communist party actually emasculated the radical movement of the next generation.

I wasn't worrying very much about where I was going in the 1930s. I was too busy. Then came a crisis, a turning point for me. The late Judge Theodore Rosen offered me a job as head of Probation and Parole for the city of Philadelphia at a salary of $8,000 a year. Now believe me, in 1938 that was a fortune. I was also to have a visiting lectureship at the University of Pennsylvania which would pay about $2,400, and on top of that I was to have a weekly column in the Philadelphia *Ledger* on how to keep your kiddies out of trouble. So altogether I would be making about $12,000. Philadelphia was less than two hours from New York, with all the concerts, theaters, and so forth. It was very tempting.

I could see myself with a house in the beautiful Philadelphia suburbs and money in the bank. I also could see myself saying, "I'd better not risk this job or this setup. After all, I can do more for the cause by stimulating my students than by taking chances myself. I can make speeches and write papers full of double-talk and put the real message between the lines or in the footnotes. Then I can flap my angelic wings and tell myself I'm really putting out dynamite."

Of course, this is so much jazz. Can you live your life between the lines or in footnotes? It doesn't work that way. Once you're on top you want to stay there. You learn to eat in very good restaurants, to fly first class. The next thing you know these things are essential to you. You're imprisoned by them.

You hear people say, "After I make my pile I'm going to do all the things I want to do." It never happens, because by that time you're a different person. Like the poor executives who put off that trip to Paris for years and years. By the time they get there they have stomach ulcers so they sit in the best French restaurants eating cornflakes.

I'd seen this kind of thing happen to men I knew—including labor leaders who were once lean, hungry young agitators and were now fat-bellied and fat-headed. So I turned down the Philadelphia job—and I've said No to some other tempting offers since then for the same reasons. I decided I'd do the organizing myself.

I knew it would be tough. You have to remember that concepts which are accepted today were considered wildly radical then—for instance, the idea that the local people have the intelligence and the ingenuity to work out their own problems. And it was heresy to tell them, "The hell with charity—the only thing you get is what you're strong enough to get, and so you'd better organize."

This is what I said when I went into "Back of the Yards" in Chicago. This was Upton Sinclair's *Jungle.* This was not the slum across the tracks. This was the slum across the tracks from across the tracks. Also, this was the heart, in Chicago, of all the native fascist movements—the Coughlinites, the Silver Shirts, the Pelley movement. Lots of people can tell you what was in my mind at the time. Boy, there are pages in criminology textbooks on my philosophy of "grassroots wholism." I don't know what that is. I went in there to fight fascism; delinquency was just incidental, the real crime was fascism. If you had asked me then what my profession was, I would have told you I was a professional anti-fascist.

In Back of the Yards, I never appealed to people on the basis of abstract values the way some civil-rights leaders do today. Sure, everybody's against sin but you're not going to get off your prat to do anything about it. To the Catholic priests my approach was simply this: "You're telling your people to stay out of the CIO because it's Communist-dominated"—it sure was then, in that particular union, although now it is clean of Communism—"So what do they do? They say, 'Yes, Father' and walk out of your church, and join the union. You want to know why? Because those union people are doing something about their living problems, about what they're suffering from, while you sit on your rear end in your sacristy."

In a mass organization you can't go outside of people's actual experience. I've been asked, for example, why I never talk to a Catholic priest or a Protestant minister or a rabbi in terms of the Judeo-Christian ethic or the Ten Commandments or the Sermon on the Mount. I never talk in those terms. Instead I approach them on the basis of their own self-interest, the welfare of their Church, even its physical property.

If I approached them in a moralistic way, it would be outside of their experience, because Christianity and Judeo-Christianity are outside of the experience of organized religion. They would just listen to me and very sympathetically tell me how noble I was. And the moment I walked out they'd call their secretaries in and say, "If that screwball ever shows up again, tell him I'm out."

Back of the Yards at that time was a hell hole of hate—the Poles, Mexicans, Negroes, Lithuanians, Hungarians, and Germans all hating each other and all of them hating the Irish, because the Irish were the power structure. I had a certain advantage when I went in there in being Jewish. I wasn't competing with any of these nationality groups. A lot of these people were attracted to fascists like Coughlin and Pelley. But this wasn't because they had any feelings for fascism. It was primarily because they had no way out, no direction, no instrumentality that offered any hope. So they had to have scapegoats. But once a program and a movement were developed, there wasn't any more need for scapegoats.

When people talk about Back of the Yards today, some of them use lines like "rub resentments raw" to describe my organizing methods. Now, do you think when I went in there or when I go into a Negro community today I have to tell them that they're discriminated against? Do you think I go in there and get them angry? Don't you think they have resentments to begin with, and how much rawer can I rub them? What happens is this: When you find yourself completely caught, subjugated, crushed in this kind of situation, you have a choice of two ways out: One way is to blow your top—you say, "Who ever asked me to come into this world anyway?" And you wind up killing your wife and your kids and yourself. You read about these things in the papers. The other way is what 99 per cent of the population does—you rationalize. You say, "Go fight City Hall. It's a tough world, tough for everybody. And this isn't too bad. I get my relief check regularly, and maybe my number will come up in the numbers, or my policy ticket— anyhow, it could be worse. I'm better off than that guy down the block." And you just exist. You keep all your anger, all your feelings pent up inside you.

What happens when we come in? We say, "Look, you don't have to take this; there is something you can do about it. You can get jobs, you can break these segregated patterns. But you have to have power to do it, and you'll only get it through organization. Because power just goes to two poles—to those who've got money, and those who've got people. You haven't got money, so your own fellowmen are your only source of strength. Now the minute you can do something about it you've got a problem. Should I handle it this way or that way? You're active. And all of a sudden you stand up." That's what happened in Back of the Yards.

"Let Them Call Me Rebel and Welcome..."

When you're in the field of action you have to do your thinking on the run. You don't have time to figure out whether what you're doing really makes sense. You don't acquire what the Greeks called real experience. In order to get experience out of living and action you've got to go off by yourself and digest it. Wise men in the old days knew this. So they went off into the wilderness to think for a while.

Well, my wilderness turned out to be a jail in a Middle Western city where I was organizing people living in a miserable slum. There was this police captain who was very anti-labor who figured my mere presence would contaminate his town. So whenever I walked down the main drag a squad car would pull up and I'd be invited in. They never booked me—just tossed me in the clink for safekeeping. I got used to it. I'd say to the jailer, "Will you please phone my hotel and tell them to expect a late arrival."

I had a very good deal in that jail—I didn't suffer at all. I had a private cell; they treated me very nicely.

Now there's no place that is better designed for reflective thinking and writing than a jail. Usually when I have to write I look for every possible excuse. I suddenly remember phone calls I haven't made. I'd better look at the papers and so forth. But in jail the situation is exactly reversed. The only way you can escape is mentally. So you're attracted to writing. It becomes a compulsion.

I wrote my book *Reveille for Radicals* in that jail. Sometimes the jailers would tell me to get out when I was in the middle of a chapter. I'd tell them, "I don't want to go now; I've got a couple of hours' more work to do." This really confused them. But after a while they got used to it.

Then the police captain started visiting me and we'd get into long conversations. You know, in the end he and I became buddies and he stopped having me picked up. If he hadn't done that, I'm sure I'd have written another book. But anyhow I have always been grateful to him for giving me a chance to digest my experiences. And I began to see then that the status quo is the greatest ally of the revolutionary.

If you study history you can see that no revolution ever got off the ground until the status quo performed the essential service of taking the leader or the organizer out of action. He'd never do it voluntarily.

Think of what that first jail experience during the Montgomery bus strike did for Martin Luther

King. That was when he decided to go all-out for total integration. And he was a very different man after the Birmingham experience, as he wrote in his *Letter from a Birmingham Jail.* He gained a much wider perspective on the sanctity of man-made laws. He came to understand that the well-wishers who say, "I approve of your objectives but not your tactics," are an anchor around your neck. He saw that revolutionary changes never occur without conflict because even a nonviolent protest is bound to produce a violent reaction.

The time I spent in jail did a lot to help me work out my own philosophy. Of course other events played a part too. I guess the most important ones were very intimate things. You see I've had more than my share of personal tragedy —with the people close to me, that I loved dearly. Death has not been a stranger to me.

And I have learned one lesson, I learned it in my belly, the astonishing lesson that I wasn't going to live forever. Now this may sound like a very simple thing, but there are very few people who realize that they're going to die someday. Intellectually they know it, but they go on saving for their old age and so forth. After the full realization, on a gut basis, that I was going to die, my whole life changed. I was confronted with the question, "What's the meaning of my life, since I'm here just so long a period of time?" I've never been able to answer that question. I don't ever expect to be able to answer it. But I know that once you reach that point of accepting your own death, you no longer care much whether you're important or not important. I've frequented the cemeteries too long—I know that that's it.

Some people say that my orientation is basically Marxist. Others say that the Industrial Areas Foundation is a front for the Roman Catholic Church. One guy said I was a Marxist who was subsidized by the Roman Catholic Church or the Presbyterian Church, and who used the tactics of a Capone mobster. It's an interesting combination, to say the least.

Of course, I'm not a Marxist. But will I accept certain things out of Marxism? Certainly. Out of the Communist Manifesto I'll take a public-school system, a graduated income tax. Does this make me a Marxist? Do I believe in the greater good for the greater number? Yes, I guess you could call me an urban Populist. My philosophy is rooted in an American radical tradition, not in a Marxist tradition.

I rarely reply to critics. The reason is not the obvious one—that if I were to spend my time replying to critics I wouldn't have time to do anything else. The real reason is this, and I try to get it across to my staff: once you become concerned about critics, subconsciously it's going to affect your actions. Instead of taking the kind of direct actions and thinking the way you're thinking now, you're going to start pausing and wondering, "What is *Harper's Magazine* going to think about it? What is the *Christian Century* going to say?" And the hell with them, you know. I told Silberman when he first came in to write about us in *Fortune*, "I don't care what you write. It isn't going to make a bit of difference. Who reads *Fortune* in Woodlawn anyway? So the critics are going to read it? They don't count."

I don't know whether there's an afterlife or not—nobody's ever given any evidence one way or the other, and I don't expect they ever will. But I don't care what people think about me in this one. One of the worst crimes that's been committed on us in quoting that line from Shakespeare about who steals my purse steals trash, but he who takes my reputation takes everything. This is a damnable lie. There's been more corruption because people were concerned about their reputations rather than their purse. I think a concern for your reputation is one of the worst prisons you can have. I had a give-and-take with some of Joe McCarthy's henchmen on this. I told them, "Go ahead, call me up, smear me. You think I give a good goddam about it?" And they knew I meant it. So they backed off. I was never called. In my book, the Eleventh Commandment is something from Tom Paine: "Let them call me rebel and welcome, I feel no concern from it; but I should suffer the misery of devils, were I to make a whore of my soul. . . ."

The Status Quo to the Rescue

The biggest change I saw in the first twenty years or so that I was involved in social action is in the role of the churches. Back in the 1930s and '40s an organizer might expect to get some help from the CIO or from a few progressive AFL unions. There wasn't a church in sight. But in the 1960s they really moved into the social arena, the political arena. They took over the position organized labor had a generation ago. They were the big dominant force in civil rights.

For instance, in Kansas City, Missouri, our whole project was financed, sponsored, and underwritten by the Episcopal Church, the Catholic Church, the Presbyterian Church. There wasn't a union in sight.

The same way in Rochester, New York. The Area Council of Churches raised the money we needed to do a job there.

Let me tell you about Rochester, which is probably the most extreme example of benevolent paternalism in this country. In an interview I called it "a Southern plantation transplanted to the North." Their press—which consists of two newspapers that are both owned by one chain—let out howls of provincial self-righteous indignation. "Smugtown U.S.A." is a good name for the place.

But the race riots in the summer of '64 gave them a bad shock. A race riot is an ugly, terrifying mass madness. It's an unreasoning, hysterical stampede of hate and violence which leads to looting and killing and leaves both sides numbed, shamed, guilty, and scared. A riot can happen wherever a mass of people feel utterly trapped, where they have no hope, no future. So they explode almost in a death agony.

Before the long hot summer of '64, the *Wall Street Journal* predicted that Woodlawn, in Chicago, would be one Negro community where there would be no race riots. They were right.

This is not because the Negroes in Woodlawn don't have grievances. They have plenty. But they also have a mass organization—which the IAF helped set up—so that the people have achieved an identity. They have unity and power and they have been able to score victories.

Of course, this is why the churches and the Negro leaders in Rochester asked us to come there. The power structure wasn't happy about the idea. In fact they tried every possible dodge to forestall it. They suddenly brought in the Urban League, which was an unfair decoy move. It put the Urban League in what was almost an Uncle Tom position. The City Fathers seized upon an inexplicable—but very timely for them —statement by Roy Wilkins from the head office of the NAACP saying that Rochester had made great strides in correcting discriminatory practices. Thirty-five thousand Negroes in Rochester don't seem to agree with Mr. Wilkins. It's peculiar too that the local NAACP decided by unanimous vote to join in asking the IAF to come to Rochester.

Then some of the neighborhood houses and social agencies started denouncing us. This reminded me of the days in the late 1930s when the CIO was organizing steel companies in upstate New York. The Wagner Act had forbidden employers to interfere with union organization. So instead they invented something that got to be known as the Mohawk Valley Formula. They would get the YMCA and the settlement houses and other little agencies to set up a so-called community council. When the CIO hit town they would start screaming "Reds, foreigners, agitators!" Of course the employers were supporting these outfits but they could say piously, "We're not violating the Wagner Act. We're not doing anything." Rochester in 1965 wasn't too different. Some of their social agencies denounced me and their papers pulled this phony "outsider" stuff on me. The IAF is more of an "insider" than any agency in the town. The Negro community actually invited us in. That's more than any other agency can say.

Of course, from the standpoint of an organizer, this kind of reaction from the status quo was the best "cooperation" I could have asked for. What I mean is this. A Bull Connor with his police dogs and fire hoses down in Birmingham did more to advance civil rights than the civil-rights fighters themselves. The same thing goes with the march from Selma to Montgomery. Imagine what would have happened if instead of stopping the marchers that first day with clubs and tear gas, chief state trooper Lingo had courteously offered to provide protection and let them proceed. By night the TV cameras would have gone back to New York and there would have been no national crisis to bring religious leaders, liberals, and civil-rights fighters from the North into Selma. I've always thought that just as King got the Nobel Prize there should be an IgNoble prize for people like

Sheriff Rainey of Philadelphia, Alabama Governor Wallace, and Governor Barnett of Mississippi.

You need characters like that for a very important organizing tactic which I call mass ju-jitsu. Here's how it works. In 1964 various Chicago civil-rights groups decided to stage a public-school boycott, but TWO (The Woodlawn Organization) was undecided about joining it. They knew they could shut up every school in their neighborhood tighter than a drum. They could do this overnight, and City Hall knew it. It had taken two years of sweat and fighting and a lot of heartbreak to build this kind of organization and power. Now the question was whether TWO should join a lot of small civil-rights groups that had very little membership and no power. If they couldn't deliver, they had nothing to lose. But if TWO was mixed up in an action which didn't deliver they had plenty to lose. After all, you only have power so long as the opposition knows that you can and will do what you say you're going to do.

Now, keeping kids out of school isn't much of a trick. As far as I know, kids have never opposed a school holiday. But to make a school boycott effective you need organization and avenues of communication. Well, TWO had a long strategy session. They knew most of these little civil-rights groups didn't have any avenues of communication and practically nobody to communicate with. But in the end, TWO decided to join the school boycott. The reason was their faith that the status quo would come to the rescue—that they would provide the communications and the incentives. Sure enough. They did. The press and TV really publicized it. Every white "civic leader" that was hated by the Negroes gave out statements denouncing the boycott. The night before, the Bulldog edition of the Chicago *Tribune* carried a front-page banner headline, "SCHOOL BOYCOTT TODAY." It appeared again in the morning. You couldn't buy that kind of publicity for a million dollars. So the school boycott was a success because the status quo lived up to our expectations.

To go back a bit further, it was really the status quo that helped us organize Woodlawn in the first place. Because of the way they had been handling their urban-renewal program, the University of Chicago was bitterly hated by nearly every leader in Woodlawn. So the University of Chicago could have ruined us by simply issuing a statement endorsing me as one of their "illustrious" alumni. In that case nobody in Woodlawn would have had anything to do with me. But when the University is concerned about its real estate, or when professors are concerned about their status—they are just pieces of the status quo and they act that way. So they attacked me and all the papers blasted the hell out of me. This was wonderful for a lot of reasons. One of my problems in Woodlawn was my white skin, but after the papers attacked me a lot of Woodlawn people began saying, "If those big fat-cat downtown white papers are calling Alinsky a dangerous, no-good son of a bitch, then he must be all right."

We went through the same kind of experience with the "enlightened" press of Rochester.

The city of Rochester has a lot to learn. The most important lesson is that people don't get opportunity or freedom or equality or dignity as a gift or an act of charity. They only get these things in the act of taking them through their own efforts. Nearly every American city still needs to learn the same thing.

That's why the Poverty Program was bound to turn into a prize piece of political pornography. It's a huge political pork barrel, and a feeding trough for the welfare industry, surrounded by sanctimonious, hypocritical, phony, moralistic crap. For instance, in Chicago one of our top Poverty officials is dragging down $22,500 and before that he was making 14 grand. That's what I call really helping the poor. Directors of the Baby City Halls which are called "Urban Progress Centers" are getting about $12,400. Before that they were averaging between $8,000 and $9,000. A police detective who was making $7,000 is now a Credit Education Consultant (you figure out what that means) and he is getting $10,000. People like that really know right down to the guts of their billfold what Johnson meant by The Great Society. Across the country, City Halls have their Committees on Economic Opportunity to identify what they call positive and negative programs and leaders. Positive means you do whatever City Hall tells you to do and negative means you are so subversive that you think for yourself.

On top of that, with all that dough they go in and suffocate the opposition with payoffs, rentals, jobs, and other kinds of legalistic bribery. For instance, they'll go into a church where there's a Negro minister with some good potential for leadership. But he's having a hard struggle with his monthly budget, his mortgage payments, with this and that. They'll walk in and say, "Look, Reverend, we're going to operate a reading class, or preschool tutoring, and we'd like to rent your premises, if you can spare them"—the damn thing's empty most of the time anyway—"for two or three hundred dollars a month rent." This is really manna from heaven. Well, the minute he makes that rental deal, bye-bye Reverend. From now on he's out of the picture as far as the movement goes.

In one Eastern city there's a Poverty Mobility Project. You want to know what that is? A settlement house gets $83,000 out of the poverty program. So they take two social workers who were making about $7,000 apiece and kick them up to $8,000. That immediately saves the settlement's budget $14,000. You know, graft has many faces and the most nauseous of all is the "dedicated" one. Then, of course, when you get two social workers together you have to have a coordinator. He gets about $12,500. That leaves you $54,500 for the Mobility Project. Now, we get down to the bone. The Mobility Project is for any poor slob in a slum neighborhood who wants to go to City Hall to register a beef, or to the County Hospital, or somewhere else. So they send out one of these high-salaried human Seeing Eye dogs, to escort him there. It would be much too simple to have the party get into a taxicab and say, "Take me to City Hall"—taxi drivers know where things are, including a lot of places social workers wouldn't know about.

Do you know what being poor means? It's not very complicated. It means not having any money. One of the best poverty programs I ever heard of was in a little Italian village. One of the natives came to America and made a lot of money. He outlived all his relatives. So when he died he left all his money to his hometown. Well the mayor and the priest and a lot of their other wise men got together and tried to figure out what to do with this inheritance. In the end they decided just to divide it up and distribute it equally to everyone in the village. It came to about six or seven hundred dollars apiece. That was twenty years ago, or more. The last time I was in Europe I made a special trip to that village to find out what happened afterward. I talked to the priest and the mayor and a lot of local people. They used that money to open up little shops, or to move north to Milan or Bologna—to get away from southern Italy, which makes Appalachia look like the Gold Coast. Their lives were changed by the simple fact that they stopped being poor.

Now I'm not suggesting that the American poor sit around waiting for somebody like that Italian Santa Claus. Things don't happen that way very often in real life. The only way the poor are going to get what they need is through strong, militant organizations of their own.

This kind of organization can be built only if people are working together for real, attainable objectives. For instance, in Woodlawn, when we organized our first school boycotts back in '62, they were for very concrete objectives—for toilet paper in the schools, for better books and so forth. Basically people aren't concerned with abstract ideals. Sure, Negro parents are for a desegregated school system but, damn it, what they primarily want is to have a better-quality school right now, whether it is around the corner, whether it is segregated or not. Now it's true that they are also very much opposed to segregation in any form. But this is a more remote objective, which is probably not going to be achieved during the school lifetime of their children, who may be in the fifth or sixth grade. They'll lend moral support to the idea of desegregation. But the issue that will bring them out into meetings and into vigorous action, is to have something done about the schools which their children go to right now. Of course, this kind of approach presents a danger. One can unwittingly fall into the trap of separate-but-equal. As a matter of fact today, many white communities would be glad to make Negro schools more than equal—of better quality than their own—if only the Negroes would stay in their own communities and stop this constant pressure. This struggle has to be fought on two fronts at once.

A mass organization must be built on many different issues—housing, jobs, schools, consumer prices, representation and power at the decision-making centers, health, crime and every other aspect of life that affects the welfare and future of the local people and their children.

When there are many different objectives there is constant daily activity and a sense of purpose and action and victory. People begin trading for each other's support, and alliances are formed between groups. One says to the other, "My number-one interest is desegregation of the schools, and your number-one interest is getting rid of the dope pushers, and you over there, your number-one interest is that you're sick and tired of being bulldozed out of neighborhood after neighborhood on this urban renewal which doesn't benefit you. Well, I need your help to desegregate the schools, and you need my help to get rid of the dope pushers, and to make urban renewal a decent program for the poor as well as the others. So, let's make a deal. I'll support each one of you, and you support me." This is the stuff of which organization is made.

A big problem of the civil-rights movement is that it has been built on just one issue, so it has enlisted only people to whom civil rights is the paramount value. This is why there have been periods of inactivity and times when the leaders became the captives of the issue and its tactics rather than the masters of power strategy on a broad front. Civil-rights groups have repeatedly found themselves compelled to demonstrate, not so much because a particular situation demanded action but because action, *any action*, was essential to keep the organizations alive. Now voting rights is a big thing in Mississippi and an organization could stay alive on it. But CORE, for instance, was just a minor stockholder in Mississippi, and that's the reason CORE was demonstrating up North. They had to. But you cannot build a movement on just one issue.

It requires a certain degree of sophistication in terms of tactics to organize a community and some of the younger civil-rights leaders don't have it. It's like putting kids into a lion's cage. They know about as much as a social worker who's taken a couple of courses in what they call CO or Community Org. Every time I hear that phrase it evokes a huge Freudian fantasy.

The problem with those kids is that they always want the third act—the resolution, the big drama. They want to skip the first act, the second act, the tediousness, the listening. Actually you do more organizing with your ears than with your tongue.

Any social surgery requires the scalpel of a strong, disciplined, vital organization, which will maintain its form and force over an extended period of time.

The Achilles' Heel of the civil-rights movement is the fact that is has not developed into a stable, disciplined, mass-based power organization. This needs to be said out loud. Many of the significant victories that have been won in civil rights were not the result of mass power strategy. They were caused by the impact of world political pressures, the incredibly stupid blunders of the status quo in the South and elsewhere and the supporting climate created particularly by the churches. Without the ministers, priests, rabbis, and nuns I wonder who would have been in the Selma march. The tragedy is that the gains that have been made have given many civil-rights spokesmen the illusion that they have the kind of organization and power they need. Self-deception like this is easy to understand. But the truth is that the civil-rights organizations have always been minuscule in actual size and power. Periodic mass euphoria around a charismatic leader is not an organization. It's just the initial stage of agitation.

Belatedly many civil-rights leaders have been rudely awakened to this situation. It remains to be seen whether they have the skill, sensitivity, and above all the infinite patience they will need.

I think the civil-rights people are moving faster and deeper in the South than in the North even though it doesn't seem that way. The segregated practices in the South are a kind of public butchery. It's visible. There's bleeding all over the place. Up here we use a stiletto, it's internal bleeding, it's not visible, but it's just as deadly. Here, however, we have courts, we can operate within the law. Down South, Dr. King used the only possible tactic. In Mississippi and Alabama the law is a mockery; it's the closest thing to what it was under the Nazis. When you can commit murder with impunity, and you can't get a conviction, there's no law.

In the North you need more sophisticated tactics. Take a thing like the Christmas boycott of department stores they tried one year. Now the public today has developed a degree of immunity to picket lines—they make you a little uncomfortable but that's about all. So instead of picketing all the stores, they should have chosen just one. Now, say you're out shopping. You look at the picket line and don't even consciously think about it. But it's so much easier to cross the street where there's another store, with the same merchandise, the same prices, and no picket line. So you go across the street. What compels the first store to come to terms is not the picket line, but the increasing volume of business of its competitor. Competition is a wonderful thing.

A while back I attended an Aspen seminar, where one guy from IBM was talking about automation. All I could think of as I was listening to him was: These computers are going to put our society in a beautiful, vulnerable spot. Just equip all the people in a community with little punchers that make the same mark that Con Edison's bills have on them. Then you can say either you desegregate or we punch a hole in your cards. Those things are up for grabs, the more mechanized a society becomes.

I want to get one thing very clear. I do not do what a lot of liberals and a lot of civil-rights crusaders do. I do not in any way glorify the poor. I do not think that people are specially just or charitable or noble because they're unemployed and live in crummy housing and see their kids without any kind of future and feel the weight of every indignity that society can throw at them, sophisticatedly or nakedly. Too often I've seen the have-nots turn into haves and become just as crummy as the haves they used to envy. Some of the fruit ranchers in California steam around in Cadillacs and treat the Mexican-American field hands like vermin. Know who those bastards are? They're the characters who rode west in Steinbeck's trucks, in *The Grapes of Wrath.*

I also want to say that even though I sound anti-liberal I'm really not. The trouble with my liberal friends—and I have a lot of them—is that their moral indignation and sense of commitment vary inversely with their distance from the scene of conflict. It's like poker. You'll never find them staying till the deal's called; they'll drop out after the second card.

But I don't mean to minimize their function. I really don't. I think the agitation of the white liberals through the years prepared the climate for the reformation which you have to have before you can have a revolution. You understand I don't consider revolution a nasty bloody word. To me evolution is a chronological term for a time-span in which general changes have occurred. But the changes were caused by a series of revolutions. There is no evolution without revolutions. And there are no revolutions without conflict. And this is the line which separates liberals from radicals. A liberal is a guy who walks out of the room when a discussion turns into a fight. Of course I have to admit a lot of radicals are ex-liberals.

I can sit down and talk with sophisticated leaders in business, religion, politics, and labor without any trouble. But I have an enormous problem communicating with the academic liberals—particularly the social scientists. I'm not talking about the sociologists who have creative, seminal minds like David Riesman or Robert Ezra Park. I'm talking about the ones who are just sort of electronic breathing accessories to computers. They suffer from verbal diarrhea and mental constipation—I don't know any other way to describe it politely.

The trouble with most academicians is that if you're not down in the arena you make grave errors of judgment. So many tactics on the scene of action aren't planned or engineered. Often they're irrational. They just happen. I train our people to be comfortable and rational in dealing with irrational circumstances. I tell them, "You never have the best course of action. You always have to pick the least bad."

This is a strange new world to the academician. He is used to talking about dualism and singularism and the ethics of ends and means. Actually there's no issue on which there has been less reflective thinking than this business of means and ends. The real question has never been: Does the end justify the means? The real question is and always has been: *Does this particular end justify these particular means?* For instance, I'm not justified in getting into a car and violating the traffic laws and maybe killing someone to keep an appointment with a guy downtown on whom a hundred thousand dollars is riding, maybe my own economic survival. But if somebody next to me has a coronary, then I am justified in rolling at eighty miles an hour to a hospital. And if a cop stops me and I tell him what's what, he is going to get in front of the car with his motorcycle and turn on his siren and help me get there.

Mark Twain once said that an ethical man was a Christian holding four aces. If you've got that you can afford to be ethical. The ethics of means involves a lot of things, such as who is the judge, the times, and whether you're winning or losing.

Let's take the bomb. Let's go back to December 10, 1941, three days after Pearl Harbor, when we were completely disarmed, we had no Navy, we were worried about an invasion and bombing on the West Coast. Suppose FDR had gone on the air to say, "We have just developed a nuclear weapon and we propose to use it on Japan. Truth and justice will triumph." The people would have cheered. There wouldn't have been any ethical arguments. But by 1945, it was all over but the shouting. It was just a question of do we kill them this way or that way. We were holding four aces, we were holding twenty aces. We hadn't even started moving our troops and Air Force over from the Atlantic theater yet, because we didn't have to. Then the bomb became an ethical question.

The position you're holding has a lot to do with ethics. I remember one time I was standing in front of a tomb in Westminster Abbey. And the inscription is about a great hero of the Empire, Major André. So I think, "For godsake, that guy was a rotten spy son of a bitch." Suddenly I realized: I'm in England. He may have been this to me, but in England he was a great hero. This is not a simple deal.

I've never treated anyone with reverence. And that goes for top business magnates and top figures in the church. Some people call my irreverence rudeness and they think it's a deliberate technique. This isn't so. I believe irreverence should be part of the democratic faith because in a free society everyone should be questioning and challenging. If I had to put up a religious symbol the way some people have crucifixes, or stars of David, my symbol would be the question mark. A question mark is a plowshare turned upside down. It plows your mind so that thoughts and ideas grow.

So-called power institutions get away with a lot because they're not challenged. You see, power is not just what the status quo has, it is more in what we may think it has. It may have ten soldiers but if we think it has a thousand soldiers, then for all practical purposes the status quo has a thousand soldiers. Rarely do they have the power we think they have and it's amazing what happens when you just suddenly stand up and say, "Who do you think you are?" I had a showdown on this once in Los Angeles with Cardinal McIntyre.

This was in '49 or '50 and an organization that I'd worked with—Mexican-Americans—had elected a city councilman who refused to take the loyalty oath. McIntyre was newly arrived in Los Angeles then, and he indicated ominous times for anybody who opposed the loyalty oath. I went in to see him. In substance I said, "Look, I've been around a long time, and I'm not one of these liberals who sees the Catholic Church as a big, powerful, monolithic operation. I know what you can do and I know what you can't do. If you want to go to the mat on this, okay, let's go. We'll be glad to take you on."

The upshot was that McIntyre backed off completely.

Sometimes I'm asked about the danger of a demagogue—a dictator, a Huey Long—taking over one of our organizations. Isn't this a big risk? Actually it isn't. It's never happened in all our experience—going back twenty-five years. There are several reasons. For one thing a demagogue can only flourish in a vacuum—like Hitler. But when people are actively involved in an organization that is moving, that gives them hope for the future, a Hitler has no chance. Then too, when there is really wide participation, there is a lot of jealousy about status, everyone is watching everyone else, it's hard for anyone to push out in front—he'd be pulled back by the others. We used to be quite concerned about the danger of a demagogue but we don't worry about it any more.

What I do worry about these days is the Radical Right—specifically the John Birch Society. I've gotten into some situations where these people have really let their hair down and they are as viciously anti-Semitic and anti-Negro as the Nazis. One of their top organizers on the West Coast told me the only thing wrong with Hitler was that he let some of the Jews get away.

Now let's not underestimate this operation. It's growing. In a way this is a consequence of the bomb. But the problem isn't what the liberals are talking about or what the peace-movement people are talking about. I'm not really worried that somebody will push a button tomorrow. What we're up against is this:

Very few people, relatively speaking, grow up

—mature. They live in the kind of world they would like it to be rather than the world as it is. Now the chief difference between these two worlds is that in the one we would like it to be problems get solved. The Prince and Princess get married and live happily ever after. But the real world isn't like this. Every time you resolve a problem, you create others in the process of resolution. Even in the most successful individual psychotherapy, the analyst doesn't remove your problems; you learn how to live with them, how to handle them.

Now ever since the world began, war has provided people with the illusion of solving problems. Of course six or eight months afterward someone will say, "For God's sake, I thought we fought a war to settle that one." But while the war was happening there always seemed to be a winner and a loser.

The one big thing the bomb has done is to take away war as a solution. And it's hard for people who are not very mature to accept the kind of world where problems no longer get solved. That's what the Goldwater business was about. People can't stand this kind of world.

Let's not kid ourselves because of what happened in the '64 election. They couldn't have gotten themselves a more inept jerk than Goldwater as the candidate. But imagine if they'd had somebody with some finesse, with some ability, who didn't provide Johnson with a lot of issues (defoliation, dropping the bomb, and all the rest of that stuff), saying one thing and then denying it.

This ever-deepening frustration provides a huge tinderbox for the Radical Right. I think this mood is what causes incidents like the thirty—or more—New Yorkers who didn't bother to call the police while a girl was murdered within earshot. We had a situation like that in Los Angeles, too. This is withdrawal—the world's gotten to be too damn much; we don't know what the hell to do with it. So what do you do? You've got all these escape mechanisms, you've got a twenty-two-inch cell in a TV set to crawl into. But even there you're hit by the difference between the world as you'd like it to be and as it is. All evening on TV you can watch plays where all the good guys win and the bad guys get killed. Then you come to the ten o'clock newscast and you're punched right into the real world where the good guys get killed.

I've got a little house near Carmel, which is really a Brigadoon fantasy place where people go to get away from everything. Well, for years radio station KRML gave Carmel a special morning news report called the sunshine news, only the good news! And boy, they had to stretch to get it.

This middle-class, Madison Avenue hygienic approach to life is frightening. We're in danger of being chloroformed out of the American way of life because we're afraid of controversy. Nobody wants to be different. It's a worse threat than the bomb. We'll do it our way, with huge sleeping tablets. So we'll all die peacefully in bed. But what the hell difference does it make? When you die, you die, you know.

One thing we instill in all our organizations is that old Spanish Civil War slogan: "Better to die on your feet than to live on your knees."

Social scientists don't like to think in these terms. They would rather talk about politics being a matter of accommodation; a cooperative search for the common good; negative self-interest versus public-regarding ethos; consensus—and not this conflict business. This is typical academic drivel. How do you have consensus before you have conflict? There has to be a rearrangement of power and then you get consensus.

My liberal academic friends also like to talk about automation and millions of school dropouts who are unemployable and a contracting economy and the uncertainties of the international situation, and so forth. Now I don't know what the consequences of all these things will be and nobody else seems to. But I do know one simple thing—regardless of what the situation is, people will not be able to do anything constructive, anything in the true democratic spirit for themselves, unless they have the power to cope with the situation whatever it may be and whenever it occurs.

So I'm just holding at that point. Just build the organization and cross each bridge as we come to it.

If man has opportunity and the power to use that opportunity, then I'll bet on him to cross any bridge, no matter how tough or seemingly hopeless it may look. As a matter of fact, I've already bet my life on it.

Introduction to Part Two

In Rochester, New York, under Alinsky's guidance, a community organization calling itself FIGHT (Freedom, Integration, God, Honor, Today) chose as its main target the city's industrial giant, Eastman Kodak. The battle was memorable for many reasons but chiefly because it was his first opportunity to test out a weapon for which he sees a bright future—the use of stock proxies to challenge corporate power.

Following Rochester, Alinsky and his staff responded to appeals for help from Buffalo, Kansas City and a dozen or so other cities—and from the California vineyards where two Alinsky-trained organizers, Cesar Chavez and Dolores Huerta, formed a grape pickers' union and organized a nationwide consumers' grape boycott. One of his liveliest encounters was in Oakland, California where the City Council met in emergency session to ban him from the city following the announcement that he was about to arrive at the invitation of the Presbyterian Church. He made something of a triumphal entry across the Bay Bridge, armed with a Chicago birth certificate and a U.S. passport, and trailed by a small army of TV cameras and newspaper reporters. "The welcoming committee of Oakland police looked and felt pretty silly," he recalls.

Though still anathema to conservative Americans, Alinsky's ideas had gained increasing acceptance in the closing years of the 'sixties. His old adversary (and alma mater), the University of Chicago, had turned into a staunch friend and ally of The Woodlawn Organization, which it had once deemed an arch-foe. And on campuses from coast to coast he had become something of a folk hero. Much of his time was spent crisscrossing the country to prod, challenge and often outrage college audiences. More suprisingly, corporate executives and church conventions in mounting numbers welcomed his abrasive presence. But Alinsky keeps his guard up, "When I feel they are trying to seduce me, then I let them have it. And, bang! I'm back in the gutter again—where I belong."

In the spring of 1968 he announced that he and the small staff of the Industrial Areas Foundation would no longer roam the nation stirring up trouble in person. Instead they would set up an institute where organizers from communities across the country would be trained to operate on their home grounds. Some would, of course, be potential leaders of the poor and black. But a prime goal of the Institute would be to train organizers of the middle class. Within a few weeks, the Institute was swamped with applications.

Alinsky's homecoming evoked a mixed reaction from Chicagoans, for his announcement also included a message for the natives. "Chicago is too quiet," he cheerfully told interviewers. "It's become a desert so far as dissent goes." He forecast, among other things, that Mayor Daley's martial preparations for the Democratic National Convention would produce bloody conflict and hand the 1968 election to the Republicans. (Such statements led local rightwingers to burn him in effigy at the corner of State and Madison.)

As an antidote to local apathy he launched an anti-pollution drive which moved into high gear after the city was suddenly darkened by what one columnist called "a blanket of floating filth."

When Mayor Daley denied that the pollution problem was serious, Alinsky rejoined, "What the hell does he breathe with—his ears."

In the autumn of 1969, Alinsky and I met again to talk about the cataclysmic events of the past four years and particularly about his new mission of organizing the middle class. Like the preceding narrative, the one that follows was distilled out of many hours of wide-ranging conversation.

M.K.S.

Tactics for the Seventies

It doesn't seem like it's been four years since the last time we talked at length. It's all gone by like a shot. That's a hell of a way to put it when you remember Dallas, Memphis, Los Angeles, and other places. Well, I suppose these are rough times and anyone in a fight who is really doing something becomes a target. I've had my sticky scenes, a couple really up-tight, but you don't worry about it because if you do you've got no business being in the arena to begin with, and after all, none of us are going to come out of life alive anyway. I get these threats all the time—from the Klan, the Minutemen, the Young Republican Clubs of California, the Birchers, any time I land in what I call my kooky country.

Maybe with luck I still have ten good productive years ahead of me. So I keep thinking—what's the best use I can make of them? I've come to see very clearly that this country is predominantly middle-class economically. Almost four-fifths of our people are in that bracket, so that's where the power is. Hell, we would have to be blind not to see that this is where organization has to go. This became plenty clear when we were fighting Eastman Kodak and went into the proxy deal. We had to go to the churches and the other middle-class groups that owned stocks and had proxies they could turn over to us. That's where we found the strength to carry on the fight for the organization of the poor in Rochester. We saw the same thing when Cesar Chavez staged the grape boycott—a middle-class consumer boycott. So that's the job we've got to take on and train organizers to do.

One thing I've learned in spades—though I didn't want to accept it for a long time—is this: organization doesn't come out of an immaculate conception. It takes a highly trained, politically sophisticated, creative organizer to do the job. And it can't be done just on a local basis because the problems today are regional and national so you need a national power organization. But to build it you've got to have pieces to put together, local pieces. And to build them you've got to have trained organizers. That's why I'm doing what I'm doing now—training the organizers.

Another thing that matters is that this is a corporate economy. That's where the power—the political and economic power—is. Now where are you going to find the strength to make the corporations use that power for the things that need to be done? Suppose you could get all the blacks in the country, all the Mexican-Americans, all the poor whites, all the Puerto Ricans organized. And suppose some genius formed them into a coalition. That would be maybe 55 million people by the end of the 1970s. But the population will be around 225 million by then. So the poor will still be a minority who need allies and they'll have to find supporters among the three-quarters of our people who are middle-class.

I'm including here the lower-lower middle class, making up to about $7,500—the employed poor, the "have a little, want more" group. Then you have the lower middle class at around nine, ten, or eleven thousand a year. Like the working poor they're in hock up to their ears with time payments. So are the middle middle class, making $15,000 a year or so. In some ways the middle-class groups are more alienated, more out of the scene even than the poor. There aren't any special funding programs for them. They don't have special admissions to universities. They don't have a special anything except getting constantly clobbered by taxes and inflation.

These people are just thrashing around in their own frustrations. They couldn't be effective allies for anyone because they're overcome, completely confused by their own problems. So they fall back on two common clichés. One is: "I don't care to be involved." Or maybe someone else will call himself a "concerned citizen." This is really saying the rest of the citizens are not concerned, so they're not citizens at all. When masses of people disengage in this way it's a perfect setup for the extreme Right, for the dictators whose pitch is, "Just follow me and all will be well."

How do you organize these frustrated middleclass people? You find out what they care about, what they are worried about, and you organize them around these issues. Now inflation is not an issue. Crime is not an issue. *It only becomes an issue when you can do something about it.* That's what the organizer is for.

Actually there are very few real issues and every organizer knows this. For instance, life itself is what people want most. But it's not an issue because there's nothing you can do about it. We have to accept the fact that we're all going to die. I suppose you could make an issue out of death in some spots around Los Angeles, but we're not talking about organizing nuts. When people discover that through organization they have the power to do something, what was just a big sad scene breaks down into specific issues.

Take the war. The Vietnam Moratorium gave millions of people a way to do something about this. Of course, there are middle-class people who are not against war so you don't talk about it to them. The issues for them would be a constellation of other things—maybe taxes, gun control, pollution, schools, zoning, pornography.

Look at a community like Cicero, Illinois. An organizer could draw a crowd there in a hurry if he went in and said, "Let's keep the blacks out of our neighborhood." Well, you can't do that because you can't compromise on the basic principles of a free and open society such as equality and justice. But you don't start out right off the bat by saying, "Racists are banned from this organization, and we're going to fight for the right to bring blacks in here." If you do that, they'll all walk out on you and you'll have nobody to communicate with. So you avoid the race issue. You leave it alone. You know that once you have them organized on other issues, the situation will change. This is not just theory. I've seen this operate ever since the early days of Back of the Yards. Sooner or later, even the low-income whites in a black-hating community find out that in order to get the things they want—to be safe in the streets and their homes for instance—they've got to make a deal, they need support. So they begin to say, "We're not talking about this race business, just man to man. You support us for this, and we'll support you for that." A deal is based on a common need for each other—you care for the other guy when you need him. Blacks and whites are going to get together on common gut desires and not on what is called conscience. We've seen what conscience has produced over the centuries, or specifically since the Civil War.

The whole concept of organizing people on an altruistic basis, the way white liberals tried to do something for the blacks, is a lot of crap. This just isn't the way life is. Invariably, the right things get done for the wrong reasons. So the organizer looks for wrong reasons to get right things done.

These are some of the things we're teaching at the Institute. I'd planned originally to locate it in Berkeley. But we didn't get the support—the financial support—from the churches out there that we'd hoped for. So we were more or less stalled when I got a call from Gordon Sherman, the president of Midas Muffler. I'd never met him. All I knew about him was that he was a big corporation executive in town whose hobbies include playing the oboe, raising rare birds and orchids, mountain-trout fishing, and the United Jewish Appeal. He offered us about a half-million dollars, no strings attached except it's got to be in Chicago. He wants things to happen in this town the way I do. He's what the kids call a beautiful person. He is that. He practically set up the whole Chicago Businessmen's Committee Against the Vietnam War and he's helping support the Ralph

Nader operation, the war against pollution, the Moratorium, you name it. Then, the Rockefeller Foundation gave us a quarter of a million dollars, again without strings. And we got a grant of $35,000 from another foundation which doesn't want to be named. The Presbyterian Church gave us $50,000. Then we have the fees from my lectures which are quite substantial and all go to IAF—Industrial Areas Foundation. So we can give scholarships to the students who need them —the course runs fifteen months.

We're enrolling a very mixed bag of students. Right now we have a Roman Catholic priest, a Presbyterian minister, a social worker, and a former steel worker. We have a Mexican-American who has organized in California; a Puerto Rican from the lower West Side of New York; an Indian sent by American Indians United; a black who has been organizing from Virginia to Pittsburgh, both in and out of jail and in the Georgia State Penitentiary; a white girl from Connecticut who has been organizing around Hartford; a white Jesuit seminarian from the Boston area, and so it goes. They're all as different from each other as could be and yet they all have one thing in common: they want change and want to know how to get it.

How do we find these people? Some of them come to us, of course. Then too, we operate like a major-league ball club—we scout the sandlots looking for the troublemakers. Maybe we'd find you agitating for better schools in your community. We'd watch you and talk to you to find out whether you have an open mind, whether you're a free person, not one imprisoned by a doctrine. We'd also want to make sure you have a very good sense of humor, that you're not one of those dour, dedicated people who long to wear a hair shirt.

Then one thing we'd want to be sure of is that when you finish training you have a scene to go back to. We're not going to waste our time training someone who's going to wind up at a foundation as a consultant. When I hear the word "consultant" I always think about the guy who had a castrated dog. Every time a bitch in heat would pass by, this dog would try to break the window to get out. One day this fellow had a friend over who saw this performance. The friend says, "I don't get it. Why does your dog act this way, because if he did get out he couldn't do anything." The dog's owner answered with great indignation, "You don't understand. My dog is a consultant."

Suppose one of our men is trying to organize a community on the issue of water pollution—that's got a lot of people very upset in the suburbs where you turn on a faucet and nothing comes out but foam from detergents. It's a good issue but I can't tell you what tactics he'd use because in organization you are always improvising. For instance, The Woodlawn Organization—TWO —in Chicago got Mayor Daley to deal with them after they threatened to tie up all the rest rooms at O'Hare—keeping all the booths occupied. O'Hare is one of Daley's sacred cows. Another time TWO people piled rats on the steps of City Hall. Daley got that message too. The Northwest Community organizations in Chicago filled an old truck with garbage and dumped it on an alderman's lawn. They got better garbage pickups after that.

The only thing the poor have as far as power goes is their bodies. When TWO has a bunch of housing complaints they don't forward them to the building inspector. They drive forty or fifty of their members—the blackest ones they can find—to the nice suburb where the slumlord lives and they picket his home. Now we know a picket line isn't going to convert the slumlord. But we also know what happens when his white neighbors get after him and say, "We don't care what you do for a living—all we're telling you is to get those niggers out of here or you get out." That's the kind of jujitsu operation that forces the slumlord to surrender and gets repairs made in the slums.

Let me give you another kind of example. I was lecturing at a college which is run by a very conservative, almost fundamentalist Protestant denomination. Afterward some of the students came to my motel to talk to me. Their problem was that they couldn't have any fun on campus. They weren't permitted to dance or smoke or have a can of beer. I had been talking about the strategy of effecting change in a society and they wanted to know what tactics they could use to change their situation. I reminded them that a tactic is doing what you can with what you've got. "Now what have you got?" I asked. "What do they permit you to do?" "Practically nothing," they said, "except—you know—we can chew gum." I said, "Fine. Gum becomes the weapon. You get two or three hundred students to get two packs of gum each, which is quite a wad. Then you have them drop it on the campus walks. This will cause absolute chaos. Why, with five hundred wads of gum I could paralyze Chicago, stop all the traffic in the Loop." They looked at me as though I was some kind of a nut. But about two weeks later I got an ecstatic letter saying, "It worked! It worked! Now we can do just about anything so long as we don't chew gum."

When you think about organizing today, especially the middle class, you don't think about community just in geographic terms. People are drawn together by common interests, not because they live near each other. Take the question of taxes—how do you make a real issue out of that? Well, one idea I have is that there should be a graduated sales tax just the way we have a graduated income tax. Why should the poor and the working poor and the lower- and middle-income classes pay the same sales taxes for the essentials of life as the upper middle class and the rich? I'm suggesting that the Internal Revenue

Service issue special ID cards for people with incomes less than $10,000. When they buy something they show the ID card and pay no sales tax at all. There's no means test here. If you're too proud to show your ID card, why you can just pay the tax. People in the middle middle class would have a different kind of card and would pay double tax. The upper middle class and the rich would have no ID cards and would pay triple the regular sales tax. We plan to try out something like this locally in the spring, maybe in New York State.

There are plenty of other ways to use the tax issue. For instance, clergy, university, and foundation people are exempt from the federal tax on air travel. Why shouldn't other citizens in lower income groups be exempt too? At the other end, why not charge a much higher tax to people traveling on expense accounts—this would be one way for IRS to cut into the expense-account gravy train.

Another tactic which we've already tried out is Proxies for People. We started this in Rochester with Eastman Kodak. The leading churches in the city who held Kodak stock turned over their proxies to FIGHT—the organization we helped set up in the ghetto there. This turned out to be our major weapon in getting Kodak to deal with FIGHT and to set up a training and job program for blacks.

The Kodak story got considerable national press publicity. And suddenly we were deluged with mailbags full of stock proxies in different companies. People wrote saying, "I've got some money to invest; what stock should I buy? What proxies do you want?" This response gave us a glimpse of how the middle class could really organize to accomplish something instead of just signing petitions or buying full-page ads in the *New York Times*. People suddenly saw that you can do something with proxies besides throw them in the wastebasket or sign them and mail them back to the company.

We plan to get into the corporate arena by setting up a separate organization called Proxies for People. We will ask all the liberals in America to mail us stock proxies. Organized stockholders can actually go to annual meetings, not just to ask questions about profits and about hiring policies or just to demand to know what the company is doing about pollution, but wielding proxy power to change corporate policy and practice.

Some corporate executives are getting to be pretty sophisticated. I was having a couple of scotches with one of them the other day and he showed me the blueprints of a new factory. "Boy," he said, "we have a really 'with it' architect. On the main floor he's designed a sit-in room for demonstrations. It'll have a coffee urn and lots of chairs that aren't too comfortable." Then he turned to me, looking quite serious, and asked, "Are you really going ahead with this Proxies for People thing?" I assured him that we are.

I've also thought of going to Ford and the other

foundations and saying, "Look, we're not asking for a penny. But we notice your portfolio contains thousands of shares in companies that have a lot to say about how this country is run. You claim you're committed to a better society. So give us your proxies and we'll take care of the rest." The labor-union welfare funds are loaded with stocks and proxies, too. Let's put them on the spot.

I'd like to see the campus activists get into this too, instead of just chasing Dow Chemical recruiters off campus. Let them set up student-faculty committees and demand control of all the proxies in the university's investment portfolio. That would really be a way to raise all kinds of hell and get some results.

The college kids, of course, are mostly the upper and middle middle class. When you start thinking about organizing the lower middle class, you're dealing with something that's different in many ways, so the tactics will be different.

The average policeman is typical of the lower middle class. He's married, he and his wife go to church, he has a small house, a car, and a library full of installment-payment books. His job and a fireman's are a little more romantic than a garbage collector's. Still he knows it's the kind of job most people look down on. He has some opportunity for advancement. But he sees that in the last fifteen or twenty years anyone who really went upstairs in the department was a college graduate or a professional of some sort. So the fact that he never went to college is very important to him. He hopes his kids will go.

Then his whole world goes smash. The kids who are rampaging on campus don't seem to know the value of anything. They never had to work. They go around yelling slogans about Che Guevara—and he doesn't know who Che was, except some damn Red—or some Chinaman named Mao. He thinks these kids should get their goddam asses beaten.

He finds he isn't respected anymore. In the old days he could walk any place, go into a dark alley, and except in rare instances no one would dare assault him. If you were a cop-killer, then God help you. The department would go out and get you. In Chicago, if a cop was killed the mobs would send the word back, "We didn't have anything to do with it." Or, "We already took care of the guy who did it." Because when a cop's been killed the heat's on. Well, the policeman doesn't have that kind of protection anymore. And he has no status, no rationale for being. The way he looks at it, why are his hands tied when nutty kids occupy buildings and take out confidential files? From his point of view they're defecating on his most precious values. It's not just the police who feel this way.

One day when I was lecturing at a big university, there was some kind of uproar. A Marine recruiter was driven off campus. I didn't see it happen, in fact I didn't hear about it till dinner

that evening. I got back to my hotel around one
o'clock and went into the bar for a nightcap.
The place was empty except for the bartender
and a Marine master sergeant in dress uniform,
with a chestful of campaign ribbons and hash
marks up to his elbows. He was sitting way down
at the end of the bar, putting away one drink
after another and crying audibly. It was very up-
setting—a middle-aged man, very masculine, to-
tally demoralized and crying.

I asked the bartender, "What's up?" He
shrugged his shoulders and said, "He's been that
way for the last three hours." I took my drink
and sat down next to the sergeant and said,
"Come on, buddy, things can't be that tough."
Pretty soon he started talking. It turned out he
was the recruiting sergeant who had been driven
off campus. His eyes were filled with complete confusion—it wasn't just that he was pretty
well stoned. He kept saying, "I don't get it. I
don't know what's happening. I was at Iwo Jima.
I was at Tarawa. I've seen my buddies alongside
me getting their guts blown out; they died for
these punks. And now I go on a college campus
and you'd think I was a goddam Nazi, the way
they treat me. I just don't understand what's happening to the world."

This is how the policeman feels. So what does
he do to have some rationale for living? Well, the
super-duper patriots in the community who are
screaming for law and order seem to be about the
only people who have any respect for him. So he

gets active in the American Legion, in the John Birch Society maybe. This gives him some status.

We've been contacted by a small group of policemen about going into our training program, men we think can become organizers in their communities and at the same time get some real status for themselves.

We've been talking with some black policemen also. In a lot of ways the black policeman is having the same trouble as the black intellectual. On the surface the black intellectual has never had it so good. If he has a master's degree he'll be offered a job that a white Ph.D. couldn't get. But at the same time he's trapped. He's joined the other side, moved away from his own people. So he may work out his guilt by militant rhetoric, by becoming what I call an Uncle Tough-Talk or the black in the gray flannel dashiki.

The black policeman is in an even worse spot. He's assigned to the ghetto, where he's not only a pig but a black pig. The hate expressed toward black cops in many ghettos is much worse than the feeling toward white cops. One black officer we had in training said to me, "We're in a real bind, a real box. Which comes first, our job or our people? Well, we have to be with our people. We couldn't stand it otherwise and after a while our lives wouldn't be worth a nickel in the neighborhood." In other words, if they don't express some hostility to whites their own people will denounce them.

The answer isn't just to organize black police

unions which would give them better opportunities for promotion. Our idea is to train them to become leaders among their own people, to help them develop mass power organizations that will fight for better housing, schools, and so forth. Our program with this group has been suspended at this point. Maybe this is the wrong time to start.

One of the biggest problems we face on the whole race issue is a complete collapse of communications. This goes both ways and all kinds of walls are up now which in some ways are as bad as the old segregationist walls. This is very important because it doesn't make any difference what ideas come up on the white side or on the black side; so long as we can't communicate with each other except in what I would call a crippled communication, then we're in for real trouble. You get a combination of screwed-up white and black neurotics whose vocabulary is all crapped up with masochism and sadism, and it's a goddam mess.

Right now you have the blacks saying, "Whitey, get lost, stay away from us, do your own thing with your own people." So I accept the fact that today, in spite of my record, my white skin disqualifies me from the kind of direct organizing work I've done in Chicago and Rochester and other ghettos.

In this climate, I'm convinced that all whites should get out of the black ghettos. It's a stage we have to go through. I'd like to see legislation enacted making it mandatory for all white businessmen and slum landlords in the ghettos to sell their stuff to blacks within an eighteen-month period. If they haven't done it by that time, then let the government come in—just like Urban Renewal—appraise their properties and businesses, condemn them, and then turn around and help blacks buy them with special funding or low-interest-rate loans. This is what they say they want. And until the blacks have the experience of being exploited by their own people as they were by the whites, this will be a constant thorn, a constant source of anti-Semitism because so many of the businessmen are Jews who stayed on after they moved their homes out of the ghetto.

I'm not saying this is any real answer for the blacks. You set up a black-owned gas station and what have you got? Four jobs. Or a black-owned liquor store or grocery store. This will accomplish nothing except maybe psychologically. A small businessman can't compete in terms of prices and service. If the blacks are to get a piece of the economic pie they've got to become part of the corporate economy. This was one of the unexpected things that came out of the battle with Eastman Kodak in Rochester. The big gain was that Xerox got into the picture. They've helped set up a black-owned company which is a subcontractor, making a product for Xerox. That's going to work out in terms of a lot of jobs. That's getting into the corporate economy, which is where the jobs and money are.

Sure, the blacks' demand for separatism is wrong. It's one of the irrationalities you have to accept, part of life, part of growing up. After all, we've made black the color of everything ugly and shameful. Nobody is ever pinkmailed, he's blackmailed. Nobody is ever kicked out of a club on a blue list, it's a blacklist. We use black for mourning, for funerals; we've made it the color of tragedy, of evil. We talk about black days of infamy. So it's natural for them to react by saying black is beautiful. In the end they'll see that black is beautiful and ugly. White is beautiful and ugly. Every color is beautiful and ugly.

Though a lot of people don't understand this, the Black Panthers are not all-out separatists. They have some awareness that you must work with others. So they have more potential than most of the militants. But they need new tactics. I'd like to see them mount a big offensive to get the drug racket—the pushers—out of the ghettos. Suppose the Panthers were to say, "One way the blacks are kept down is by getting them hooked. We are going to get those pushers out if they have to be carried out." Now what would happen? For one thing the Panthers would have a plausible explanation of why the police keep hounding them, because obviously the drug traffic can't keep going without big payoffs to the police. And the Panthers would begin to communicate with a lot of middle-class families— white and black—who are worried stiff about their own kids and drugs. I think this is the ideal assignment for the Panthers. What other organization is really fighting the drug racket? Who else is going to have the courage or the lack of prudence to take on the Mafia except a bunch of eighteen-year-old Panthers who are ready to die for a cause? If they did this I think you'd see a big switchover in attitudes toward them. The police would have to back off and there would be a constructive force going in terms of the whole black-white relationship.

You can't force people to love each other, so at this point we can't talk about integrated communities. I still stand by the testimony I gave before the U.S. Civil Rights Commission five years ago. Then I defined a racially integrated community as a chronological term timed from the entrance of the first black family to the exit of the last white family. While the blacks are moving in and the whites are moving out it's integrated. The only way you can have integration is for the whole city to open up, almost simultaneously. Otherwise, when just one community opens up, whether by black initiative or blockbusting, the pressure is so great that the community just turns over.

It's ironic that the blacks themselves are pushing now for apartheid. This makes the racist whites very comfortable. When I was in the deep South a few months ago I ran into a KKK guy I'd met once before. He came up to me and said, "Mr. Alinsky, I want you to know you're wrong about we Southerners. You've always called us racists and bigots. But I want to tell you that first of all I'm an American and I believe everybody has the right to live the way he wants to. And if those blacks want to live separate and eat separate, I'll fight to the death for their right to do it." I remember looking at him and thinking to myself, "Why, you son of a bitch. Your organization ought to send a big contribution to these black separatists. Boy, have they taken you and your kind off the hook. Before all this separatist stuff you guys were always squirming trying to figure out answers because you were trapped with our American political traditions of equality and all of your church stuff about love and dignity. Now these separatists have given it to you on a silver platter. You don't even have any hangups. You just stand there and look at me and hand me all of this patriotic shit. Christ, life can really get screwed up."

There's been a complete loss of communication between blacks and whites. If a white guy says something really far out, your reaction is, "You ought to go to Bellevue and get a spinal test." But if it's a black man, you listen politely and say, "That's a very interesting approach." You're so scared of being tarred with the label of racist or bigot. Actually, what you're doing is even worse. You're treating him like a problem child. It's paternalism, condescension.

After one of my campus lectures, a really militant black got up, just oozing hostility. "Mr. Alinsky," he said, "I want to ask you a question. But first I want to know, will you be speaking for all the rest of the honkies?" "Okay," I said, "I'll answer your question. But first I want to know, are you speaking for all the rest of the niggers?" Then I walked to the end of the platform and looked at all the blacks who were sitting together. "Look, get this straight," I said, "all of you blacks. One: I am your *equal*. Two: I am not one of those guilt-ridden, screwed-up, neurotic liberals you characters have been dealing with. Like the ones in the San Francisco Bay area who went around wearing big buttons saying HONKIES FOR HUEY during the Huey Newton trial. If I were in a jam I wouldn't expect you to wear big buttons saying NIGGERS FOR SAUL. And you know damn well you wouldn't do it. So don't give me any of that crap."

There was a moment's silence. Then the fellow who had asked the question said, "Well what I meant was—is your answer going to be typical of the white position?" I answered, "Is your question going to be typical of the black position? Now let's talk." We had quite a good discussion and the white students all of a sudden began sitting up like people.

Sometimes I think my mission at a lot of these universities is to liberate the whites. Often, they tell me, they will be talking with a black friend and he will suddenly freeze up and get a completely impassive look on his face, because three other black students come strolling by and are watching him. So he has to revert to his hostile role. This can't go on. It's too damn stupid.

There are certain things that are the same when you are organizing whether it be the poor, the Eskimos, the blacks, the Mexican-Americans, or the American middle class. But there are differences too. One of the big problems with organizing the middle class here is that they've got real hang-ups against being rude or vulgar or what they would call creating a scene.

The trouble is that to organize people there's got to be action and all action on a minute-to-minute basis is rude and involves making a scene. You can't have the manners of a cocktail party when you storm into a Senator's office, or City Hall.

To give you an example, I was flying into New York from San Francisco during an air traffic jam-up. We were due at five-thirty but didn't make it in until about eleven o'clock that night. We'd only eaten one meal all day. The hotel we went to had kept the dining room open late but they'd run out of entrees. So I found myself with a grilled cheese sandwich and a cup of coffee. Some people sitting at a table near me ordered griddle cakes. The waitress brought them but not the syrup and butter. Every time they said, "Miss," she would say, "Wait a minute," and the cakes were getting colder and colder. I tapped one of them on the shoulder and asked if they

wanted the butter and syrup. He said, yes, we
would appreciate it. So in a loud voice I yelled
across the floor, "Hey get off your goddam ass
and bring the butter and syrup right now."
Which she did. These people were so horrified
that they kept telling the waitress they didn't
know me, had nothing to do with me, that they
were not responsible for the scene. Of course
while they were saying this they ate their butter
and syrup on the griddle cakes.

To give you a different example, last year one
of the top editors of the *Louisville Courier-Jour-
nal* was telling me that his paper was the only one
in the United States which printed the complete
text of the Walker Report about the Democratic
National Convention in my city—Chicago. In
full, with all the four-letter words all over the
front page, page two, page three, and so on. That
day all hell broke loose. Churches calling, organizations, and irate citizens, all saying, "How could
you do that—print those four-letter words all
over the place?" "By the afternoon," he went on,
"I was saying over the phone, 'Look, we made a
bad policy mistake. I apologize—this paper will
never do it again.' Finally I went home to dinner.
And a young college senior who was visiting us
starts in on me again saying, 'Don't you know
that there are certain things you just don't do?'
By this time I'm utterly defeated. Now she gets
up from dinner in her evening gown. She has a
formal date and he shows up in a tuxedo. The
two of them go out. Well, it so happens that our

dog unloaded right in front of the door and she steps into it. The next thing I hear is the cultured, well-modulated voice of this young lady saying, 'Oh shit, I just stepped in the googoo.' How the hell do you straighten these people out?"

It's very hard to try to get across how an organizer works—being loose and free, not really knowing himself what the issues are going to be. He knows that in life you go with the action and that you consciously look for hooks and handles that you can grab hold of, that you can twist and turn and pull and get the reaction that is so important in building a power organization. People ask me, "So you're going to organize the middle class? How are you going to start? What are you going to do?" How the hell do I know? All I know is what every really good organizer knows —you react to all the action with a reflex: "How do I use this to build the organization?" Maybe a year from now I can tell you what really happened with the proxies and all the other ideas we have now.

As you know, in Chicago we're starting to organize around the issue of air and water pollution. We'll be taking on some more of Mayor Daley's sacred cows—the corporations like Commonwealth Edison and Inland Steel that are mainly responsible for pollution—which really should be spelled pollootion because it amounts to looting the public. If Commonwealth Edison complains that it will take a long, long time to get rid of their coal-burning, air-polluting generators, then I say—the hell with them. Let's take the company over in public ownership and make those changes in eighteen months instead of eighteen years. Of course, I expect people to start yelling "socialism" when they hear this. This is a word with a lot of different definitions according to who's talking about what. The characters who live in swanky Lake Forest call it socialism when the government's welfare programs give money to the poor. But you don't hear them bellyaching when they ride along freeways built 90 per cent with federal money or when they latch onto a nice fat defense contract. When the other guy gets money, it's socialism; but when you get it, that's "cooperation between the private and public sectors."

One of the problems in any community is that the people who make the most noise intimidate the others like the Birchers in some middle-class suburbs. Lone individuals are afraid to stand up against them. But the minute they organize and feel they have some support, they stop being scared.

It takes a certain something that most people don't have to stand up when you're all alone. I learned this when I was ten or eleven, living in a Jewish slum. Next to us was a Polish community. And talk about the race issue, gangs, and turfs— you couldn't find more hate than there was between Poles and Jews. If any of us crossed 16th

Street we got the shit beaten out of us. And we did the same to the Poles if we caught them in our neighborhood. There used to be mass invasions, like war, like a pogrom.

One day one of my friends came to us all bruised. He'd been jumped by three kids in the Polish section. So naturally we went on the hunt and found a couple of Poles. We were merrily beating them up when the police suddenly appeared and arrested all of us. They took us down to the station house and called our mothers. The mothers came in screaming about how their kids had brought disgrace on their families. Who ever heard of good Jewish boys being arrested? And they promised the police sergeant their boys would be punished plenty when they got home.

My mother didn't take me home. Instead she took me to the rabbi—I was very devout up to about the age of twelve. The rabbi started telling me how wrong I was and I defended myself. "They beat us up," I said. "So we beat them up. That's the American way. It's also in the Old Testament: an eye for an eye, a tooth for a tooth. Beat the hell out of them. That's what everybody does."

The rabbi answered, "You think you're a man because you do what everybody does. Now I want to tell you something the great Rabbi Hillel said: *Where there are no men, be thou a man.* I want you to remember that."

I've never forgotten it.

Format by C. Linda Dingler
Set in Janson
Composed, printed and bound by Colonial Press Inc.
HARPER & ROW, PUBLISHERS, INCORPORATED